# COOKING ON A BUDGET
# quick and easy

# COOKING ON A BUDGET
## quick and easy

easy to buy, prepare and cook

*p*

This is a Parragon Book
First Published in 2005

Parragon
Queen Street House
4 Queen Street
Bath BA1 1HE
United Kingdom

This edition designed by Fiona Roberts
Photography and text by The Bridgewater Book Company Ltd.

ISBN: 1-40544-886-5

Printed in China

NOTE
This book uses metric and imperial measurements. Follow the same units of measurement
throughout; do not mix metric and imperial. All spoon measurements are level: teaspoons are
assumed to be 5 ml and tablespoons are assumed to be 15 ml. Unless otherwise stated, milk
is assumed to be full fat, eggs and individual vegetables such as potatoes are medium, and
pepper is freshly ground black pepper.

The times given for each recipe are an approximate guide only because the preparation times
may differ accordingly to the techniques used by different people and the cooking times may
vary as a result of the type of oven and other equipment used.

Recipes using raw or very lightly cooked eggs should be avoided by infants, the elderly,
pregnant women, convalescents and anyone suffering from an illness. Pregnant
and breast-feeding women are advised to avoid eating peanuts and peanut products.

# contents

# introduction

When it comes to food it sometimes seems that we have to choose between the inexpensive but time – consuming and the costly but convenient. This is not the case – it is possible to prepare and cook delicious and nourishing meals without spending hours slaving over a hot stove or ripping the family budget to shreds. In fact, it's astonishingly easy and all it really needs is a slight adjustment in the way you think about cooking quickly – and the recipes in this book, all of which can be prepared from scratch and cooked in under an hour.

We tend to believe that only expensive cuts of meat, such as steak and pork fillet, can be cooked quickly and to some extent this is true, but if you shift your perspective slightly, you will discover that it's not invariably the case. Meatballs and stir-fries, for example, are among the speediest, easiest and most economical dishes to prepare and taste just great. Chicken is always good value for money and it's a well-kept secret that the cheaper, dark meat has much more flavour than the more expensive breast portions. In any case, it makes budgetary sense to buy a whole chicken and cut it into pieces yourself than to buy already prepared portions.

Nutritionists advise us to eat five portions of fruit and vegetables a day and because they cost much less than meat and poultry, the bank manager would probably agree. In every sense it is worth considering the occasional vegetarian option, especially if you bear in mind that seasonal vegetables are usually much less expensive than non-seasonal, imported ones. Moreover, most vegetables taste better and retain more nutrients when they are cooked quickly. Also, don't overlook those natural 'convenience' foods like eggs and cheese. They can form the basis of numerous delicious dishes, can be made in moments and cost little more than a few pennies.

## Shopping

Plan your menus in advance, write a shopping list and stick to it. Try to avoid dashing around the supermarket in your lunch hour, grabbing the first thing you see or, even more expensive, stocking up on ready-meals. Frozen and chilled dishes are rarely as good as the pictures on the packaging, often fail to satisfy the appetite and never taste as delicious as home cooking. Ready-made sauces don't really save very much time, are usually packed with added flavourings, colourings and preservatives and cost a silly amount of money

| BUDGETING GUIDE | |
|---|---|
| £ | Bargain |
| ££ | Budget |
| £££ | Economical |

compared with, say, a can of tomatoes, a few herbs and an onion or a little flour, butter, milk and grated cheese. You can rustle up a much tastier tomato or cheese sauce at home in no time at all for a fraction of the cost.

*There are lots of quick dishes to make using the simplest of ingredients*

### Time and Money

■ Scissors are often quicker to use than a knife when chopping some ingredients, such as herbs and bacon.

■ Many people have kitchen equipment that they hardly every use. If you have a food processor or blender, take advantage of its time-saving qualities for chopping, slicing, shredding, grating and making breadcrumbs (don't throw away stale bread - crumb it instead).

*Delicious meals can be created in minutes, even on a budget!*

■ It's quicker and easier not to peel some vegetables and if you cook them with their skins, they retain more nutrients too.

■ When baking potatoes, push a metal skewer through the centres. This speeds up the cooking time and therefore lowers energy bills.

■ When buying chicken, always choose fresh. If you buy a frozen bird, you may be paying for as much as ten per cent water.

■ In the case of meat products, such as sausages, cheapest is rarely the best value. Quite apart from the disappointing flavour, they tend to burst during cooking unless you cook them very gently and slowly. They often leak large amounts of fat so you are left with a rather unappetizing end product.

# instant tomato sauce

- makes about 400 g/14 oz
- prepared in: 5 minutes
- cooks in: 4 - 6 minutes

**1 tbsp vegetable oil**
**2 garlic cloves, crushed**
**400g/14 oz canned chopped tomatoes**
**dash of Tabasco sauce**
**salt and pepper**

1 Heat the oil in a frying pan and cook the garlic, stirring frequently, for 2-3 minutes. Add the tomatoes and their can juice and bring to the boil, stirring. Boil over a high heat, stirring and scraping up the sediment from the base of the pan, for 2-3 minutes until thickened.

2 Remove the pan from the heat, season to taste with salt and pepper and stir in the Tabasco.

# soups, snacks & sides

Most people know that home-made soup is an economical

dish, but you maybe surprised to learn that you don't have to cook

it for hours and it still tastes wonderful. So too, do the other

dishes in this chapter, whether you serve them as starters,

light meals or accompaniments.

# speedy broccoli soup

■ serves 6
■ prepared in 10 mins
■ cooks in 20 - 25 mins

**350 g/12 oz broccoli**
**1 leek, sliced**
**1 celery stick, sliced**
**1 garlic clove, crushed**
**350 g/12 oz potato, diced**
**1 litre/1¾ pints vegetable stock**
**1 bay leaf**
**freshly ground black pepper**
**crusty bread or toasted**
  **croûtons, to serve**

1 Cut the broccoli into florets and set aside. Cut the thicker broccoli stalks into 1-cm/½-inch dice and put into a large saucepan with the leek, celery, garlic, potato, stock and bay leaf. Bring to the boil, then reduce the heat, cover and simmer for 15 minutes.

2 Add the broccoli florets to the soup and return to the boil. Reduce the heat, cover and simmer for a further 3–5 minutes, or until the potato and broccoli stalks are tender.

3 Remove from the heat and leave the soup to cool slightly. Remove and discard the bay leaf. Purée the soup, in small batches, in a food processor or blender until smooth.

4 Return the soup to the saucepan and heat through thoroughly. Season to taste with pepper. Ladle the soup into warmed bowls and serve immediately with crusty bread or toasted croûtons.

1                    1                    1

# carrot & orange soup

££

- serves 6
- prepared in 10 mins
- cooks in 20 mins

**55 g/2 oz butter**
**2 onions, grated**
**salt and pepper**
**700 g/1 lb 9 oz carrots, grated**
**1 large potato, grated**
**2 tbsp grated orange rind**

**1.4–1.7 litres/2½–3 pints boiling**
**water**
**juice of 1 large orange**
**2 tbsp chopped fresh parsley,**
**to garnish**

1 Melt the butter in a large, heavy-based saucepan. Add the onions and cook over a medium heat, stirring constantly, for 3 minutes. Sprinkle with a little salt, add the carrots and potato, then cover, reduce the heat and cook for 5 minutes.

2 Stir the orange rind into the saucepan, then add enough boiling water to cover. Return to the boil, cover and simmer briskly for 10 minutes. Add the orange juice.

3 Remove the saucepan from the heat and leave to cool slightly, then pour into a food processor and process until a smooth purée forms. Alternatively, use a hand-held electric blender to purée the soup in the saucepan. Return the soup to the saucepan, adding a little more boiling water if it is too thick. Return to the boil, taste and adjust the seasoning if necessary and ladle into warmed soup bowls. Garnish with chopped parsley and serve immediately.

# tomato & red pepper soup

**££**

- serves 4
- prepared in 15 mins
- cooks in 35 mins

**2 large red peppers**
**1 large onion, chopped**
**2 sticks celery, trimmed and**
  **chopped**
**1 garlic clove, crushed**
**600 ml/1 pint vegetable stock**
**2 bay leaves**
**800 g/1lb 12 oz canned plum**
  **tomatoes**
**salt and pepper**
**2 spring onions, finely shredded,**
  **to garnish**
**crusty bread, to serve**

1 Preheat the grill to hot. Halve and deseed the peppers, arrange them on the grill rack and cook, turning occasionally, for 8–10 minutes until softened and charred.

2 Leave the peppers to cool slightly, then carefully peel off the charred skin. Reserving a small piece for garnish, chop the pepper flesh and place it in a large saucepan.

3 Mix in the onion, celery and garlic. Add the stock and the bay leaves. Bring to the boil,

cover and simmer for 15 minutes. Remove from the heat.

4 Stir in the tomatoes and transfer to a food processor or blender. Process for a few seconds until the mixture is smooth, then return it to the saucepan.

5 Season the soup with salt and pepper to taste and heat for 3–4 minutes until piping hot. Ladle into warm bowls and garnish with the reserved pepper, cut into strips, and the shredded spring onion. Serve with crusty bread.

1

2

4

# chicken noodle soup

**£££**

- serves 4 - 6
- prepared in 10 mins
- cooks in 25 mins

1 sheet of dried egg noodles
from a 250 g/9 oz packet

1 tbsp oil

4 skinless, boneless
chicken thighs, diced

1 bunch spring onions, sliced

2 garlic cloves, chopped

2 tsp finely chopped fresh
root ginger

900 ml/1½ pints chicken
stock

200 ml/7 fl oz coconut milk

3 tsp red curry paste

3 tbsp peanut butter

2 tbsp light soy sauce

1 small red pepper, chopped

60 g/2 oz frozen peas

salt and pepper

1 Put the noodles in a shallow dish and soak in boiling water as the packet directs.

2 Heat the oil in a large preheated saucepan or wok.

3 Add the diced chicken to the pan or wok and fry for 5 minutes, stirring until lightly browned.

4 Add the white part of the spring onions, the garlic and ginger and fry for 2 minutes, stirring.

5 Stir in the chicken stock, coconut milk, red curry paste, peanut butter and soy sauce.

6 Season with salt and pepper to taste. Bring to the boil, stirring, then simmer for 8 minutes, stirring occasionally.

7 Add the red pepper, peas and green spring onion tops and cook for 2 minutes.

8 Add the drained noodles and heat through. Spoon the chicken noodle soup into warmed bowls and serve with a spoon and fork.

# chickpea & tomato soup

**££**

- serves 4
- prepared in 5 mins
- cooks in 15 mins

2 tbsp olive oil

2 leeks, sliced

2 courgettes, diced

2 garlic cloves, crushed

800 g/1 lb 12 oz canned chopped tomatoes

1 tbsp tomato purée

1 bay leaf

850 ml/1½ pints vegetable stock

400 g/14 oz canned chick peas, drained and rinsed

225 g/8 oz spinach

salt and pepper

Parmesan cheese, freshly grated, to serve

1 Heat the olive oil in a large saucepan, then add the leeks and courgettes and cook them briskly for 5 minutes, stirring constantly.

2 Add the garlic, tomatoes, tomato purée, bay leaf, vegetable stock and chick peas.

1

3 Bring the soup to the boil and simmer for 5 minutes.

4 Shred the spinach finely, add to the soup and cook for 2 minutes. Season to taste.

2

5 Discard the bay leaf. Serve the soup immediately with freshly grated Parmesan cheese and warm sun-dried tomato bread.

**NOTE:** If you invest in a block of fresh Parmesan it can be stored in the fridge for a long period and thus becomes an economical ingredient.

4

# tuscan bean soup

(£)

- serves 6
- prepared in 15 mins
- cooks in 20 mins

300 g/10½ oz canned cannellini
  beans, drained and rinsed
300 g/10½ oz canned borlotti
  beans, drained and rinsed
about 600 ml/1 pint chicken or
  vegetable stock
115 g/4 oz dried conchigliette or
  other small pasta shapes
4–5 tbsp olive oil
2 garlic cloves, very finely
  chopped
3 tbsp chopped fresh flat-leaf
  parsley
salt and pepper

1 Place half the cannellini and half the borlotti beans in a food processor with half the stock and process until smooth. Pour into a large, heavy-based saucepan and add the remaining beans. Stir in enough of the remaining stock to achieve the consistency you like, then bring to the boil.

2 Add the pasta and return to the boil, then reduce the heat and cook for 15 minutes, or until just tender.

3 Meanwhile, heat 3 tablespoons of the oil in a small frying pan. Add the garlic and cook, stirring constantly, for 2–3 minutes, or until golden. Stir the garlic into the soup with the parsley. Season to taste with salt and pepper and ladle into warmed soup bowls. Drizzle with the remaining olive oil to taste and serve immediately.

1　　　　2　　　　3

# brown lentil & pasta soup

££

- serves 4
- prepared in 5 mins
- cooks in 25 mins

4 rashers streaky bacon,
  cut into small squares
1 onion, chopped
2 garlic cloves, crushed
2 celery sticks, chopped
50 g/1¾ oz farfalline or
  spaghetti, broken into small
  pieces

400 g/14 oz canned brown
  lentils, drained
1.2 litres/2 pints hot vegetable
  stock
2 tbsp chopped fresh mint
fresh mint sprigs, to garnish

1

1 Place the bacon in a large frying pan together with the onion, garlic and celery. Dry fry for 4–5 minutes, stirring, until the onion is tender and the bacon is just beginning to brown.

2 Add the pasta to the frying pan and cook, stirring, for 1 minute to coat the pasta in the fat.

2

3 Add the lentils and the vegetable stock and bring to the boil. Reduce the heat and leave to simmer for 12–15 minutes, or until the pasta is tender but still firm to the bite.

4 Remove the frying pan from the heat and stir in the chopped fresh mint. Transfer the soup to warmed soup bowls, garnish with fresh mint sprigs and serve immediately.

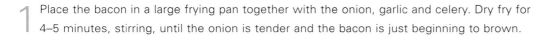

3

# bean burgers

- serves 4
- prepared in 15 mins
- cooks in 20 mins

1 tbsp sunflower oil, plus
  extra for brushing
1 onion, finely chopped
1 garlic clove, finely chopped
1 tsp ground coriander
1 tsp ground cumin

115 g/5 oz button
  mushrooms,
  finely chopped
425 g/15 oz canned pinto or
  red kidney beans, drained
  and rinsed

2 tbsp chopped fresh
  flat-leaf parsley
plain flour, for dusting
salt and pepper
burger buns and salad,
  to serve

1 Heat the oil in a heavy-based frying pan. Add the onion and cook, stirring occasionally, for 5 minutes, until softened. Add the garlic, coriander and cumin and cook, stirring frequently, for 1 minute more. Add the mushrooms and cook, stirring constantly, for 4–5 minutes until all the liquid has evaporated. Transfer the mixture to a bowl.

2 Place the beans in a small bowl and mash with a potato masher or fork. Stir the beans into the mushroom mixture with the parsley and season to taste with salt and pepper.

3 Form the mixture into 4 portions and shape each into a round, flat patty. Dust with flour. Brush the patties with oil and cook under a preheated grill for 4–5 minutes on each side. Serve immediately in burger buns with salad.

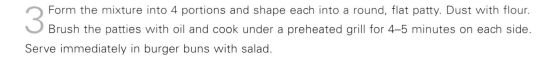

# grilled potatoes with lime

- serves 4
- prepared in 10 mins
- cooks in 15 - 20 mins

450 g/1 lb potatoes,
   unpeeled and scrubbed
3 tbsp butter, melted
2 tbsp chopped fresh thyme
salt and pepper
paprika, for dusting

**LIME MAYONNAISE**
150 ml/5 fl oz mayonnaise
2 tsp lime juice
finely grated rind of 1 lime
1 garlic clove, crushed
pinch of paprika
salt and pepper

1 Cut the potatoes into 1 cm/1/2 inch thick slices.

2 Cook the potatoes in a saucepan of boiling water for 5–7 minutes – they should still be quite firm. Remove the potatoes with a perforated spoon and drain thoroughly.

3 Line a grill pan with kitchen foil. Place a layer of potato slices on the foil.

3

4 Brush the potatoes with the melted butter and sprinkle the thyme on top. Season to taste with salt and pepper.

5 Cook the potatoes under a preheated medium grill for 10 minutes, turning once during cooking.

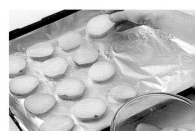
4

6 Meanwhile, prepare the lime mayonnaise. In a small bowl, combine the mayonnaise, lime juice, lime rind, garlic and paprika, and season with salt and pepper to taste.

7 Dust the hot potato slices with a little paprika and serve them hot with the lime mayonnaise.

6

# tomato rice

£

- serves 4
- prepared in 15 mins
- cooks in 15 - 20 mins

6 tomatoes
1 tbsp oil
1 large onion, finely chopped
1 tbsp curry paste
1 tsp ground coriander
1 tsp ground cumin
salt and pepper
175 g/6 oz basmati rice
600 ml/1 pint chicken or
   vegetable stock
2 tbsp chopped fresh coriander
8 poppadums, to serve

1 Cut 4 of the tomatoes in half and cut out the cores, then reserve. Roughly chop the remaining tomatoes and reserve until required.

2 Heat the oil in a large saucepan. Add the onion and fry until softened. Add the reserved tomato halves, curry paste, ground coriander, cumin and salt and pepper to taste and cook for 2–3 minutes.

3 Add the rice and stir-fry for 2–3 minutes. Add the stock and simmer for 10–12 minutes, or until the rice is tender and the tomatoes have pulped into the mixture. Remove the tomato skins where possible.

4 Mix the reserved chopped tomatoes and coriander together in a bowl and stir into the rice mixture. Serve immediately with poppadums.

2                                 3

# potato & mushroom hash

££

- serves 4
- prepared in 10 mins
- cooks in 35 mins

675 g/1½ lb potatoes, diced
1 tbsp olive oil
2 garlic cloves, crushed
1 green pepper, deseeded and diced
1 yellow pepper, deseeded and diced
3 tomatoes, diced

75 g/3 oz button mushrooms, halved
1 tbsp vegetarian Worcestershire sauce
2 tbsp chopped fresh basil
salt and pepper
fresh basil sprigs, to garnish
warm crusty bread, to serve

2

4

5

1 Cook the potatoes in a saucepan of boiling salted water for 7–8 minutes. Drain well and reserve.

2 Heat the oil in a large, heavy-based frying pan and cook the potatoes for 8–10 minutes, stirring until browned.

3 Add the garlic and peppers to the frying pan and cook for 2–3 minutes.

4 Stir the tomatoes and mushrooms into the mixture and continue to cook, stirring, for a further 5–6 minutes.

5 Stir in the Worcestershire sauce and basil and season well.

6 Transfer the hash to a warmed serving dish, garnish with the fresh basil and serve at once with crusty bread.

# tuscan bean & tuna salad

£

- serves 4
- prepared in 30 mins
- cooks in 0 mins

**1 small white onion or 2 spring onions, finely chopped**
**2 x 400 g/14 oz cans butter beans, drained**
**2 medium tomatoes**
**185 g/6½ oz can tuna, drained**
**2 tbsp flat-leaf parsley, chopped**
**2 tbsp olive oil**
**1 tbsp lemon juice**
**2 tsp clear honey**
**1 garlic clove, crushed**

1 Place the chopped onions or spring onions and butter beans in a bowl and mix well to combine.

2 Using a sharp knife, cut the tomatoes into wedges.

3 Add the tomatoes to the onion and bean mixture.

4 Flake the tuna with a fork and add it to the onion and bean mixture together with the parsley.

5 In a screw-top jar, mix together the olive oil, lemon juice, honey and garlic. Shake the jar until the dressing emulsifies and thickens.

6 Pour the dressing over the bean salad. Toss the ingredients together using 2 spoons and serve.

1          2          5

# ...ied rice

- serves 4
- prepared in 20 mins
- cooks in 10 mins

150 g/5½ oz long-grain rice

3 eggs, beaten

2 tbsp vegetable oil

2 garlic cloves, crushed

4 spring onions, chopped

125 g/4½ oz cooked peas

1 tbsp light soy sauce

pinch of salt

shredded spring onion,
   to garnish

1 Cook the rice in a pan of boiling water for 10–12 minutes, until almost cooked, but not soft. Drain well, rinse under cold water and drain again.

2 Place the beaten eggs in a saucepan and cook over a gentle heat, stirring until softly scrambled.

3 Heat the vegetable oil in a preheated wok or large frying pan, swirling the oil around the base of the wok until it is really hot.

4 Add the crushed garlic, spring onions and peas and sauté, stirring occasionally, for 1–2 minutes. Stir the rice into the wok, mixing to combine.

5 Add the eggs, light soy sauce and a pinch of salt to the wok or frying pan and stir to mix the egg in thoroughly.

6 Transfer the egg fried rice to serving dishes and serve garnished with the shredded spring onion.

# fried noodles (chow mein)

£

- serves 4
- prepared in 5 mins
- cooks in 20 mins

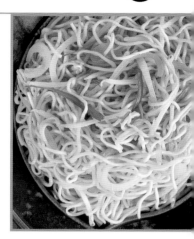

275 g/9¾ oz egg noodles
salt
3–4 tbsp vegetable oil
1 small onion, finely
  shredded
125 g/4½ oz fresh
  beansprouts

1 spring onion, finely
  shredded
2 tbsp light soy sauce
few drops of sesame oil

1 Cook the egg noodles in a wok or saucepan of salted boiling water for 4–5 minutes, or according to the packet instructions.

2 Drain the noodles well and rinse in cold water, then drain thoroughly again. Transfer to a large bowl and toss with a little vegetable oil.

1

3 Heat the remaining vegetable oil in a preheated wok or large frying pan until really hot.

4 Add the shredded onion to the wok and stir-fry for 30–40 seconds.

5 Add the beansprouts and drained noodles to the wok, stir and toss for a further 1 minute.

2

6 Add the shredded spring onion and light soy sauce and blend well.

7 Transfer the noodles to a warmed serving dish, sprinkle with the sesame oil and serve immediately.

5

# chicken & herb fritters

**£££**

- makes 8
- prepared in 10 mins
- cooks in 20 mins

500 g/1 lb 2 oz mashed potatoes,
   with butter added
250 g/9 oz cooked chicken,
   chopped
125 g/4½ oz cooked ham, finely
   chopped
1 tbsp dried mixed herbs
2 eggs, lightly beaten
salt and pepper
milk
125 g/4½ oz fresh brown
   breadcrumbs
sunflower oil, for shallow-frying
fresh parsley sprigs, to garnish
mixed salad, to serve

1 Blend the mashed potatoes, chicken, ham, herbs and 1 beaten egg together in a large bowl. Season well with salt and pepper.

2 Shape the mixture into flat patties or small balls. Add a little milk to the second beaten egg.

3 Place the breadcrumbs on a plate. Dip the patties in the egg and milk mixture, then roll in the breadcrumbs to coat them completely.

4 Heat the oil in a large frying pan and cook the fritters until they are golden brown. Garnish with a fresh parsley sprig and serve with a mixed salad.

1

2

3

# main meals

This chapter features lots of one-pot dishes, which save both time

and the cost of fuel as the whole meal is cooked at once. Others

need only rice, pasta, or potatoes, which can cook simultaneously,

to accompany them. Whichever you choose, there is a recipe to suit

all tastes from hot and spicy to mellow and melt-in-your-mouth.

# baked chicken & chips

££

- serves 4
- prepared in 10 mins
- cooks in 35 mins

| | |
|---|---|
| 4 small baking potatoes | 8 chicken drumsticks, |
| 1 tbsp sunflower oil | skin removed |
| 2 tsp coarse sea salt | 1 egg, beaten |
| 2 tbsp plain flour | 2 tbsp cold water |
| pinch of cayenne pepper | 6 tbsp dry white breadcrumbs |
| ½ tsp paprika pepper | salt and pepper |
| ½ tsp dried thyme | coleslaw, to serve |

1 Preheat the oven to 400°F/200°C. Wash and scrub the potatoes and cut each into 8 equal portions. Place in a clean plastic bag and add the oil. Seal and shake well to coat.

2 Arrange the potato wedges, skin side down, on a non-stick baking sheet. Sprinkle over the sea salt and bake in the oven for 30–35 minutes until they are tender and golden.

3 Meanwhile, mix the flour, spices, thyme, and seasoning together on a plate. Press the chicken drumsticks into the seasoned flour to lightly coat.

4 On one plate mix together the egg and water. On another plate sprinkle the bread crumbs. Dip the chicken drumsticks first in the egg and then in the bread crumbs. Place on a non-stick baking sheet.

5 Bake the chicken drumsticks alongside the potato wedges for 30 minutes, turning after 15 minutes, until both potatoes and chicken are tender and cooked through.

6 Drain the potato wedges thoroughly on paper towels to remove any excess fat. Serve with the chicken, accompanied with coleslaw.

££

# barbecued chicken legs

- serves 4
- prepared in 5 mins
- cooks in 20 mins

12 chicken drumsticks

SPICED BUTTER

175 g/6 oz butter

2 garlic cloves, crushed

1 tsp grated ginger root

2 tsp ground turmeric

4 tsp cayenne pepper

2 tbsp lime juice

3 tbsp mango chutney

crisp green seasonal salad
   and boiled rice, to serve

1 To make the Spiced Butter mixture, beat the butter with the garlic, ginger, turmeric, cayenne pepper, lime juice and chutney until well blended.

2 Using a sharp knife, slash each chicken leg to the bone 3-4 times.

3 Cook the drumsticks over a moderate barbecue for about 12-15 minutes or until almost cooked. Alternatively, grill the chicken for about 10-12 minutes until almost cooked, turning halfway through.

4 Spread the chicken legs liberally with the butter mixture and continue to cook for a further 5-6 minutes, turning and basting frequently with the butter until golden and crisp. Serve the chicken legs hot or cold with a crisp green salad and rice.

# ginger chicken & corn

**££**

- serves 6
- prepared in 10 mins
- cooks in 20 mins

3 corn-on-the-cob

12 chicken wings

2.5 cm/1 inch piece of fresh
  ginger root

6 tbsp lemon juice

4 tsp sunflower oil

1 tbsp golden caster sugar

jacket potatoes or salad,
  to serve

1 Remove the husks and silks from the corn. Using a sharp knife, cut each cob into 6 slices.

2 Place the corn in a large bowl with the chicken wings.

3 Peel and grate the ginger root or chop very finely. Place in a bowl and add the lemon juice, sunflower oil, and golden caster sugar. Mix together until thoroughly combined.

1

4 Toss the corn and chicken in the ginger mixture to coat evenly.

3

5 Thread the corn and chicken wings alternately onto metal or pre-soaked wooden skewers to make turning easier.

6 Cook under a preheated moderately hot grill or on a barbecue grill for about 15–20 minutes, basting with the gingery glaze and turning frequently until the corn is golden brown and tender and the chicken is cooked. Serve immediately with jacket potatoes or salad.

5

# chilli coconut chicken

- serves 4
- prepared in 10 mins
- cooks in 15 mins

150 ml/5 fl oz hot chicken stock

25 g/1 oz creamed coconut

1 tbsp sunflower oil

8 skinless, boneless chicken
thighs, cut into long, thin strips

1 small fresh red chilli, thinly
sliced

4 spring onions, thinly sliced

4 tbsp smooth or crunchy
peanut butter

finely grated rind and juice
of 1 lime

freshly cooked rice, to serve

spring onion tassels and fresh
red chillies, to garnish

1 Place the stock in a measuring jug and crumble the creamed coconut into the stock, stirring to dissolve.

2 Heat the oil in a large, heavy-based frying pan or a preheated wok. Add the chicken strips and cook, stirring, until golden.

3 Add the sliced red chilli and the spring onions to the frying pan and cook gently for a few minutes, stirring to mix all the ingredients.

4 Add the peanut butter, coconut mixture, lime rind and juice and simmer uncovered, stirring, for 5 minutes. Serve with rice, garnished with a spring onion tassel and a red chilli.

1  3  4

# mexican chicken

**££**

- serves 4
- prepared in 5 mins
- cooks in 35 mins

2 tbsp oil

8 chicken drumsticks

1 medium onion, finely chopped

1 tsp chilli powder

1 tsp ground coriander

425g/15 oz can chopped
  tomatoes

2 tbsp tomato paste

125 g/4½ oz frozen sweetcorn

salt and pepper

rice and mixed pepper salad,
  to serve

1 Heat the oil in a large frying pan, add chicken drumsticks and cook over a medium heat until lightly browned. Remove the chicken drumsticks from the pan and set aside until required.

2 Add the onion to the pan and cook for 3–4 minutes until softened, then stir in the chilli powder and coriander and cook for a few seconds, stirring briskly so the spices do not burn on the bottom of the pan. Add the chopped tomatoes with their juice and the tomato paste and stir well to incorporate.

3 Return the chicken drumsticks to the pan and simmer the gently for 20 minutes until the chicken is tender and thoroughly cooked. Add the sweetcorn and cook for a further 3–4 minutes. Season with salt and pepper to taste.

4 Serve with rice and mixed pepper salad.

# harlequin chicken

££

- serves 4
- prepared in 5 mins
- cooks in 25 mins

**10 skinless, boneless chicken
  thighs**
**1 medium onion**
**1 each medium red, green,
  and yellow peppers**
**1 tbsp sunflower oil**
**400 g/14 oz can chopped
  tomatoes**
**2 tbsp chopped fresh parsley**
**pepper**
**wholemeal bread and salad,
  to serve**

1 Using a sharp knife, cut the chicken thighs into bite-sized pieces.

2 Peel and thinly slice the onion. Halve and seed the peppers and cut into small diamond shapes.

3 Heat the oil in a shallow pan. Add the chicken and onion and sauté quickly until golden.

4 Add the peppers, cook for 2–3 minutes, stir in the tomatoes and parsley, and season with pepper.

5 Cover tightly and simmer for about 15 minutes, until the chicken and vegetables are tender. Serve hot with wholemeal bread and a salad.

1                    2                    4

# speedy chilli beef

**££**

- serves 4
- prepared in 15 mins
- cooks in 45 mins

3 tbsp vegetable oil
450 g/1 lb minced beef
1 onion, chopped finely
1 green pepper, seeded and
    diced
2 garlic cloves, chopped very
    finely
800 g/1 lb 12 oz canned
    chopped tomatoes

400 g/14 oz canned red kidney
    beans, drained and rinsed
1 tsp ground cumin
1 tsp salt
1 tsp sugar
1–3 tsp chilli powder
2 tbsp chopped fresh coriander

1

1 Prepare the ingredients. Heat the oil in a large flameproof casserole over a medium–high heat. Add the beef and cook, stirring, until lightly browned.

1

2 Reduce the heat to medium. Add the onion, pepper and garlic. Cook for 5 minutes, or until soft.

3 Stir in the remaining ingredients, except coriander. Bring to the boil. Simmer over a medium–low heat, stirring frequently, for 30 minutes.

1

4 Stir in the coriander just before serving.

# spicy sausage with lentils

£££

- serves 4
- prepared in 10 mins
- cooks in 25 mins

1 tbsp sunflower oil
225 g/8 oz spicy sausages,
    sliced
115 g/4 oz rindless smoked
    bacon, chopped
1 onion, chopped
6 tbsp passata
425 ml/15 fl oz beef stock

600 g/1 lb 5 oz canned
    lentils, drained and rinsed
½ tsp paprika
2 tsp red wine vinegar
salt and pepper
fresh thyme sprigs,
    to garnish

1 Heat the oil in a large, heavy-based saucepan. Add the sausages and bacon and cook over a medium heat, stirring, for 5 minutes, or until the bacon begins to crisp. Transfer to a plate with a slotted spoon.

2 Add the chopped onion to the saucepan and cook, stirring occasionally, for 5 minutes, or until softened. Stir in the passata and add the stock and lentils. Reduce the heat, cover and simmer for 10 minutes.

3 Return the sausage slices and bacon to the saucepan, stir in the paprika and red wine vinegar and season to taste with salt and pepper. Heat the mixture through gently for a few minutes, then serve immediately, garnished with fresh thyme sprigs.

# toad in the hole with onion gravy

££

- serves 4
- prepared in 5 mins
- cooks in 20 mins

8 pork sausages
25 g/1 oz dripping or lard
  or 2 tbsp vegetable oil
3 eggs
salt and pepper
300 ml/10 fl oz milk
115 g/4 oz plain flour

**ONION GRAVY**
2 tbsp sunflower oil
1 onion, chopped
1 tbsp plain flour
200 ml/7 fl oz chicken stock
1 tsp red wine vinegar
salt and pepper

1 Preheat the oven to 230°C/450°F/Gas Mark 8. Using kitchen scissors, cut in between the sausages to separate them, spread them out on a baking sheet and partially cook in the preheated oven for 10 minutes, while you make the batter. Grease the cups of a muffin tray with the dripping, and place in the oven to heat up at the same time.

1

2 Using a balloon whisk, lightly beat the eggs with salt and pepper to taste in a small bowl, then add half the milk. Sift the flour into a large bowl, add the egg mixture and stir until a smooth batter forms. Stir in the remaining milk. Remove the sausages and muffin tray from the oven and place 2 sausages in each cup. Pour in the batter and return to the oven for 10 minutes, or until the batter is puffed up and golden.

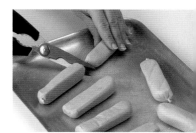

2

3 Meanwhile, make the onion gravy. Heat the oil in a large saucepan, add the onion and cook over a low heat, stirring occasionally, for 5 minutes, or until softened. Sprinkle in the flour and cook, stirring, for 1 minute. Remove the saucepan from the heat and gradually stir in the chicken stock.

4 Return to the heat and bring to the boil, stirring constantly. Stir in the vinegar and season to taste with salt and pepper. Remove the toad in the hole from the oven and serve, handing the gravy separately.

3

# neapolitan pork steaks

- serves 4
- prepared in 10 mins
- cooks in 25 mins

2 tbsp olive oil

1 large onion, sliced

1 garlic clove, chopped

400 g/14 oz canned tomatoes

2 tsp yeast extract

4 pork loin steaks, about
125 g/4½ oz each

75 g/2¾ oz black olives, stoned

2 tbsp fresh basil, shredded

freshly grated Parmesan
cheese, to garnish

green vegetables, to serve

1 Preheat the grill to medium. Heat the oil in a large frying pan. Add the onion and garlic and cook, stirring, for 3–4 minutes, or until just beginning to soften.

2 Add the tomatoes and yeast extract to the frying pan and leave to simmer for 5 minutes, or until the sauce starts to thicken.

3 Cook the pork steaks, under the preheated grill, for 5 minutes on both sides, until the meat is cooked through. Set the pork aside and keep warm.

4 Add the olives and shredded basil to the sauce in the frying pan and stir quickly to combine.

5 Transfer the steaks to warmed serving plates. Top with the sauce, garnish with freshly grated Parmesan cheese and serve immediately with green vegetables.

1     2     4

**NOTE:** If you invest in a block of fresh Parmesan it can be stored in the fridge for a long period and thus becomes an economical ingredient.

# pork chops with sage

**£££**

- serves 4
- prepared in 10 mins
- cooks in 15 mins

2 tbsp flour

1 tbsp chopped fresh sage
   or 1 tsp dried

4 lean boneless pork chops,
   trimmed of excess fat

2 tbsp olive oil

15 g/½ oz/1 tbsp butter

2 red onions, sliced into rings

1 tbsp lemon juice

2 tsp caster sugar

4 plum tomatoes, quartered

salt and pepper

1

1 Mix the flour, sage and salt and pepper to taste on a plate. Lightly dust the pork chops on both sides with the seasoned flour.

2 Heat the oil and butter in a frying pan, add the chops and cook them for 6–7 minutes on each side until cooked through. Drain the chops, reserving the pan juices, and keep warm.

2

3 Toss the onion in the lemon juice and fry along with the sugar and tomatoes for 5 minutes until tender.

4 Serve the pork with the tomato and onion mixture and a green salad.

3

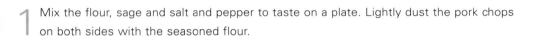
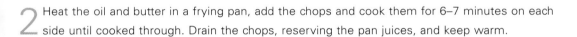

# spicy pork balls

- serves 4
- prepared in 10 mins
- cooks in 40 mins

450 g/1 lb minced pork
2 shallots, finely chopped
2 cloves garlic, crushed
1 tsp cumin seeds
½ tsp chilli powder
25 g/1 oz wholemeal
  breadcrumbs
1 egg, beaten
2 tbsp sunflower oil

400 g/14 oz canned chopped
  tomatoes, flavoured
  with chilli
2 tbsp soy sauce
200 g/7 oz canned water
  chestnuts, drained
3 tbsp chopped fresh
  coriander

1 Place the minced pork in a large mixing bowl. Add the shallots, garlic, cumin seeds, chilli powder, breadcrumbs and beaten egg and mix together well.

2 Form the mixture into balls between the palms of your hands.

3 Heat the oil in a large preheated wok. Add the pork balls and stir-fry, in batches, over a high heat for about 5 minutes or until sealed on all sides.

4 Add the tomatoes, soy sauce and water chestnuts and bring to the boil. Return the pork balls to the wok, reduce the heat and leave to simmer for 15 minutes.

5 Scatter with chopped fresh coriander and serve hot.

# lamb with mint

**£££**

- serves 4
- prepared in 10 mins
- cooks in 30 mins

2 tbsp sunflower oil
1 onion, chopped
1 garlic clove, finely chopped
1 tsp grated fresh root ginger
1 tsp ground coriander
½ tsp chilli powder
¼ tsp ground turmeric
pinch of salt
350 g/12 oz fresh lamb mince

200 g/7 oz canned chopped
   tomatoes
1 tbsp chopped fresh mint
85 g/3 oz fresh or frozen peas
2 carrots, sliced into thin batons
1 fresh green chilli, deseeded
   and finely chopped
1 tbsp chopped fresh coriander
fresh mint sprigs, to garnish

1 Heat the oil in a large, heavy-based frying pan or flameproof casserole. Add the onion and cook over a low heat, stirring occasionally, for 10 minutes, or until golden.

2 Meanwhile, place the garlic, ginger, ground coriander, chilli powder, turmeric and salt in a small bowl and mix well. Add the spice mixture to the frying pan and cook, stirring constantly, for 2 minutes. Add the lamb and cook, stirring frequently, for 8–10 minutes, or until it is broken up and browned.

3 Add the tomatoes and their juices, the mint, peas, carrots, chilli and fresh coriander. Cook, stirring constantly, for 3–5 minutes, then serve, garnished with fresh mint sprigs.

1

2

3

# spaghetti, tuna & parsley

£££

- serves 4
- prepared in 10 mins
- cooks in 15 mins

**500 g/1 lb 2 oz spaghetti**
**1 tbsp olive oil**
**25 g/1 oz/2 tbsp butter**
**black olives, to serve**
**SAUCE**
**200 g/7 oz can tuna, drained**
**60 g/2 oz can anchovies, drained**
**250 ml/9 fl oz olive oil**
**250 ml/9 fl oz roughly chopped**
   **fresh, flat-leaf parsley**
**150 ml/¼ pint crème fraîche**
**salt and pepper**

1 Cook the spaghetti in a large saucepan of salted boiling water, adding the olive oil, for 8–10 minutes or until tender. Drain the spaghetti in a colander and return to the pan. Add the butter, toss thoroughly to coat and keep warm until required.

2 Remove any bones from the tuna and flake into smaller pieces, using 2 forks. Put the tuna in a blender or food processor with the anchovies, olive oil and parsley and process until the sauce is smooth. Pour in the crème fraîche and process for a few seconds to blend. Taste the sauce and season with salt and pepper.

3 Warm 4 plates. Shake the saucepan of spaghetti over a medium heat for a few minutes or until it is thoroughly warmed through.

4 Pour the sauce over the spaghetti and toss quickly, using 2 forks. Serve immediately with a small dish of black olives, if liked.

2

3

4

# storecupboard tuna

- serves 4
- prepared in 5 mins
- cooks in 25 mins

25 g/1 oz butter, plus
  extra for greasing
25 g/1 oz plain flour
300 ml/10 fl oz milk
55 g/2 oz Cheddar cheese,
  grated
200 g/7 oz canned tuna in oil

325 g/11½ oz canned
  sweetcorn, drained
salt and pepper
2 tomatoes, thinly sliced
70 g/2½ oz plain crisps

1  Preheat the oven to 180°C/350°F/Gas Mark 4. Melt the butter in a large, heavy-based saucepan. Sprinkle in the flour and cook, stirring constantly, for 1 minute. Remove the saucepan from the heat and gradually whisk in the milk. Return to the heat, bring to the boil and cook, whisking constantly, for 2 minutes.

2  Remove the saucepan from the heat and stir in the grated cheese. Flake the tuna and add it to the mixture with the oil from the can. Stir in the sweetcorn and season to taste with salt and pepper.

3  Lightly grease a large ovenproof dish. Line the dish with the tomato slices, then spoon in the tuna mixture. Crumble the crisps over the top and bake in the preheated oven for 20 minutes. Serve.

# tuna rice

££

- serves 4
- prepared in 10 mins
- cooks in 10 mins

3 tbsp groundnut
   or sunflower oil
4 spring onions, chopped
2 garlic cloves, finely chopped
200 g/7 oz canned tuna in oil,
   drained and flaked
175 g/6 oz frozen or canned
   sweetcorn and peppers
750 g/1 lb 10 oz cold boiled rice

2 tbsp Thai fish sauce
1 tbsp light soy sauce
salt and pepper
2 tbsp chopped fresh coriander,
   to garnish

1 Heat the groundnut oil in a preheated wok or large, heavy-based frying pan. Add the spring onions and stir-fry for 2 minutes, then add the garlic and stir-fry for a further 1 minute.

2 Add the tuna and the sweetcorn and peppers, and stir-fry for 2 minutes.

3 Add the rice, fish sauce and soy sauce and stir-fry for 2 minutes. Season to taste with salt and pepper and serve immediately, garnished with chopped coriander.

# golden macaroni cheese

£

- serves 4
- prepared in 15 mins
- cooks in 20 mins

salt
200 g/7 oz dried elbow
   macaroni
1 onion, sliced
4 hard-boiled eggs, quartered
4 cherry tomatoes, halved
3 tbsp dried breadcrumbs
2 tbsp finely grated Red
   Leicester cheese

CHEESE SAUCE
40 g/1½ oz butter
5 tbsp plain flour
600 ml/1 pint milk
140 g/5 oz Red Leicester
   cheese, grated pinch
   of cayenne pepper

1 Preheat the grill to medium. Bring a large, heavy-based saucepan of lightly salted water
to the boil. Add the macaroni and sliced onion, return to the boil and cook for 8–10 minutes,
or until the pasta is tender but still firm to the bite. Drain well and tip the macaroni and onion into
an ovenproof dish.

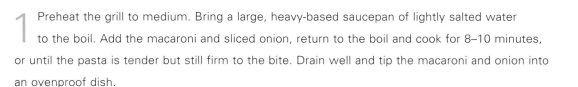

2 To make the cheese sauce, melt the butter in a saucepan. Stir in the flour and cook,
stirring constantly, for 1–2 minutes. Remove the saucepan from the heat and gradually whisk
in the milk. Return the saucepan to the heat and bring to the boil, whisking constantly. Simmer
for 2 minutes, or until the sauce is thick and glossy. Remove the saucepan from the heat, stir
in the cheese and season to taste with cayenne and salt.

1

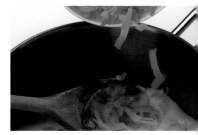

2

3 Pour the sauce over the macaroni, add the eggs and mix lightly. Arrange the tomato halves
on top. Mix the breadcrumbs with the finely grated cheese and sprinkle over the surface.
Cook under the preheated hot grill for 3–4 minutes, or until the topping is golden and bubbling.
Serve immediately.

3

# penne & butternut squash<sup>*</sup>

££

- serves 4
- prepared in 15 mins
- cooks in 30 mins

2 tbsp olive oil
1 garlic clove, crushed
55 g/2 oz fresh white breadcrumbs
500 g/1 lb 2 oz peeled and
    deseeded butternut squash
8 tbsp water
500 g/1 lb 2 oz fresh penne,
    or other pasta shapes
1 tbsp butter
1 onion, sliced
115 g/4 oz ham, cut into strips
200 ml/7 fl oz single cream
55 g/2 oz Cheddar cheese, grated
2 tbsp chopped fresh parsley
salt and pepper

1 Combine the olive oil, garlic and breadcrumbs and spread out on a large plate. Cook on HIGH power for 4–5 minutes, stirring every minute, until crisp and beginning to brown. Remove from the microwave and set aside.

2 Dice the squash. Place in a large bowl with half of the water. Cover and cook on HIGH power for 8–9 minutes, stirring occasionally. Stand for 2 minutes.

3 Place the pasta in a large bowl, add a little salt and pour over boiling water to cover by 2.5 cm/1 inch. Cover and cook on HIGH power for 5 minutes, stirring once, until the pasta is just tender, but still firm to the bite. Stand, covered, for 1 minute before draining.

4 Place the butter and onion in a large bowl. Cover and cook on HIGH power for 3 minutes.

5 Coarsely mash the squash, using a fork. Add to the onion with the pasta, ham, cream, cheese, parsley and remaining water. Season generously and mix well. Cover and cook on HIGH power for 4 minutes until heated through.

6 Serve the pasta sprinkled with the crisp garlic crumbs.

2
3
5

* This recipe is cooked in a microwave

# garlic spaghetti

£

- serves 4
- prepared in 5 mins
- cooks in 5 mins

**125 ml/4 fl oz olive oil**

**3 garlic cloves, crushed**

**salt and pepper**

**450 g/1 lb fresh spaghetti**

**3 tbsp roughly chopped fresh parsley**

1

1 Reserve 1 teaspoon of the oil and heat the remainder in a medium-sized saucepan over a low heat. Add the garlic and a pinch of salt, stirring constantly, until golden brown, then remove the saucepan from the heat. Do not allow the garlic to burn as it will taint the flavour of the oil. (If it does burn, you will have to start all over again!)

3

2 Meanwhile, bring a large saucepan of lightly salted water to the boil. Add the pasta and remaining oil, return to the boil and cook for 2–3 minutes, or until tender but still firm to the bite. Drain the pasta thoroughly and return to the saucepan.

3

3 Add the olive oil and garlic mixture to the pasta and toss to coat thoroughly. Season with pepper to taste, add the chopped parsley and toss well to coat.

4 Transfer the pasta to 4 warmed serving dishes and serve immediately.

# deep south rice & beans

££

- serves 4
- prepared in 10 mins
- cooks in 15 mins

175 g/6 oz long grain rice
4 tbsp olive oil
1 small green pepper, seeded and chopped
1 small red pepper, seeded and chopped
1 onion, finely chopped
1 small red or green chilli, seeded and finely chopped
2 tomatoes, chopped
125 g/4½ oz canned red kidney beans, rinsed and drained
1 tbsp chopped fresh basil
2 tsp chopped fresh thyme
1 tsp Cajun spice
salt and pepper
fresh basil leaves, to garnish

1 Cook the rice in plenty of boiling, lightly salted water for about 12 minutes, until just tender. Rinse with cold water and drain well.

2 Meanwhile, heat the olive oil in a frying pan and fry the green and red peppers and onion gently for about 5 minutes, until softened.

3 Add the chilli and tomatoes, and cook for a further 2 minutes.

4 Add the vegetable mixture and red kidney beans to the rice. Stir well to combine thoroughly.

5 Stir the chopped herbs and Cajun spice into the rice mixture. Season to taste with salt and pepper, and serve, garnished with basil leaves.

2            4            5

# spanish tortilla

- serves 4
- prepared in 10 mins
- cooks in 35 mins

1 kg/2 lb 4 oz waxy potatoes, thinly sliced

4 tbsp vegetable oil

1 onion, sliced

2 garlic cloves, crushed

1 green pepper, deseeded and diced

2 tomatoes, deseeded and chopped

25 g/1 oz canned sweetcorn, drained

6 large eggs, beaten

2 tbsp chopped fresh parsley

salt and pepper

2

3

4

1 Parboil the potatoes in a saucepan of lightly salted boiling water for 5 minutes. Drain well.

2 Heat the oil in a large frying pan, add the potatoes and onion and then sauté over a low heat, stirring constantly, for 5 minutes until the potatoes have browned.

3 Add the garlic, green pepper, tomatoes and sweetcorn, mixing well.

4 Pour in the eggs and add the parsley. Season to taste with salt and pepper. Cook for 10–12 minutes until the underside is cooked through.

5 Remove the frying pan from the heat and continue to cook the tortilla under a preheated medium grill for 5–7 minutes or until the tortilla is set and the top is golden brown.

6 Cut the tortilla into wedges or cubes, depending on your preference, and transfer to serving dishes. Serve with salad. In Spain tortillas are served hot, cold or warm.

# mushroom stroganoff

- serves 4
- prepared in 5 mins
- cooks in 15 mins

| | |
|---|---|
| **1 onion** | **salt and pepper** |
| **25 g/1 oz butter** | **chopped fresh parsley,** |
| **450 g/1 lb closed cup** | **to garnish** |
| **mushrooms** | |
| **1 tsp tomato purée** | |
| **1 tsp coarse grain mustard** | |
| **150 ml/5 fl oz crème fraîche** | |
| **1 tsp paprika** | |

1 Chop the onion finely. Heat the butter in a large, heavy-based frying pan. Add the onion and cook gently for 5–10 minutes, until soft. Meanwhile, trim and quarter the mushrooms.

2 Add the mushrooms to the frying pan and stir-fry for a few minutes until they begin to soften. Stir in the tomato purée and mustard, then add the crème fraîche. Cook gently, stirring constantly, for 5 minutes.

3 Stir in the paprika and season to taste with salt and pepper. Garnish with chopped parsley and serve immediately.

# midweek medley

£££

- serves 4
- prepared in 15 mins
- cooks in 20 - 25 mins

1 large aubergine

2 courgettes

6 tbsp vegetable ghee or oil

1 large onion, quartered
   and sliced

2 garlic cloves, crushed

1-2 fresh green chillies,
   seeded and chopped,

2 tsp ground coriander

2 tsp cumin seeds

1 tsp ground turmeric

1 tsp garam masala

400 g/14 oz can chopped
   tomatoes

300 ml/½ pint vegetable
   stock or water

salt and pepper

400 g/14 oz can chickpeas,
   drained and rinsed

2 tbsp chopped mint

150 ml/¼ pint double cream

1   Trim the leaf end off aubergine and cut into cubes. Trim and slice the courgettes.

1

2   Heat the ghee or oil in a saucepan and fry the aubergine, courgettes, onion, garlic and chillies over a low heat, stirring frequently, for about 5 minutes, adding a little more oil to the pan, if necessary.

3   Stir in the spices and cook for 30 seconds. Add the tomatoes and stock and season with salt and pepper to taste. Cook for 10 minutes.

3

4   Add the chickpeas to the pan and cook for a further 5 minutes.

5   Stir in the mint and cream and reheat gently. Taste and adjust the seasoning, if necessary. Transfer to a warm serving dish and serve hot with plain or pilau rice, or with parathas, if preferred.

5

# pasta & chilli tomatoes

££

- serves 4
- prepared in 10 mins
- cooks in 15 mins

275 g/9½ oz fresh pappardelle
3 tbsp groundnut oil
2 garlic cloves, crushed
2 shallots, sliced
225 g/8 oz green beans, sliced
100 g/3½ oz cherry tomatoes, halved
1 tsp chilli flakes
4 tbsp crunchy peanut butter
150 ml/5 fl oz coconut milk
1 tbsp tomato purée
sliced spring onions, to garnish

1 Bring a large, heavy-based saucepan of lightly salted water to the boil. Add the pasta, return to the boil and cook for 5–6 minutes.

2 Heat the groundnut oil in a preheated wok or large frying pan. Add the garlic and shallots and stir-fry for 1 minute.

3 Drain the pasta thoroughly. Add the green beans and drained pasta to the wok and stir-fry for 5 minutes. Add the cherry tomatoes to the wok and mix well.

4 Mix the chilli flakes, peanut butter, coconut milk and tomato purée together in a bowl.

5 Pour the chilli mixture over the noodles, toss well to combine and heat through. Transfer to warmed serving dishes and garnish with sliced spring onions. Serve immediately.

3        3        5

# mexican chilli corn pie

**££**

- serves 4
- prepared in 25 mins
- cooks in 20 mins

1 tbsp corn oil

2 garlic cloves, crushed

1 red pepper, deseeded and diced

1 green pepper, deseeded
and diced

1 celery stick, diced

1 tsp hot chilli powder

400 g/14 oz canned chopped
tomatoes

325 g/11½ oz canned sweetcorn,
drained

215 g/7½ oz canned kidney beans,
drained and rinsed

salt and pepper

2 tbsp chopped fresh coriander

fresh coriander sprigs, to garnish

tomato and avocado salad, to serve

**TOPPING**

125 g/4½ oz cornmeal

1 tbsp plain flour

½ tsp salt

2 tsp baking powder

1 egg, beaten

6 tbsp milk

1 tbsp corn oil

125 g/4½ oz mature Cheddar
cheese, grated

3

2

4

1 Heat the corn oil in a large frying pan and gently fry the garlic and the diced peppers
and celery for 5–6 minutes until just softened.

2 Stir in the chilli powder, tomatoes, sweetcorn, beans and seasoning. Bring to the boil
and simmer the mixture for 10 minutes. Stir in the coriander and spoon into an ovenproof dish.

3 To make the topping, mix together the cornmeal, flour, salt and baking powder. Make a well
in the centre, add the egg, milk and oil and beat until a smooth batter is formed.

4 Spoon over the pepper and sweetcorn mixture and sprinkle with the cheese. Bake in
a preheated oven, at 220°C/425°F/Gas Mark 7, for 25–30 minutes, until golden and firm.

5 Garnish with the coriander sprigs and serve the pie immediately with a tomato and avocado salad.

# desserts

Just because you're short of time there is no excuse for

omitting dessert or serving boring old ice cream. From Sticky

Sesame Bananas to Quick Tiramisù, there are fabulous sweet treats

with an individual touch that will cost little in time or money.

Who could possibly resist?

# sticky sesame bananas

**££**

- serves 4
- prepared in 10 mins
- cooks in 20 mins

**4 ripe medium bananas**
**3 tbsp lemon juice**
**115 g/4 oz caster sugar**
**4 tbsp cold water**
**2 tbsp sesame seeds**
**150 ml/5 fl oz low-fat natural**
**fromage frais**
**1 tbsp icing sugar**
**1 tsp vanilla essence**
**shredded lemon rind**
**and shredded lime rind,**
**to decorate**

1 Peel the bananas and cut into 5 cm/2 inch pieces. Place the banana pieces in a bowl, spoon over the lemon juice and stir well to coat – this will help prevent the bananas from discolouring.

2 Place the sugar and water in a small pan and heat gently, stirring constantly, until the sugar dissolves. Bring to the boil and cook for 5–6 minutes until the mixture turns golden brown.

3 Meanwhile, drain the bananas and blot with kitchen paper to dry. Line a baking sheet or board with baking paper and arrange the bananas, well spaced apart, on top.

4 When the caramel is ready, drizzle it over the bananas, working quickly because the caramel sets almost instantly. Sprinkle the sesame seeds over the caramelised bananas and set aside to cool for 10 minutes.

5 Mix the fromage frais with the icing sugar and vanilla essence.

6 Peel the bananas away from the paper and arrange on serving plates.

7 Serve the fromage frais as a dip, decorated with the shredded lemon and lime rind.

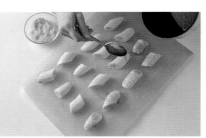

1    3    4

# quick syrup sponge*

£

- serves 4
- prepared in 11 mins
- cooks in 9 mins

140 g/5 oz butter or
  margarine
4 tbsp golden syrup
6 tbsp caster sugar
2 eggs
125 g/4½ oz self-raising
  flour

1 tsp baking powder
about 2 tbsp warm water
custard, to serve

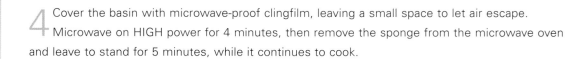

1 Grease a 1.5-litre/2¾-pint heatproof basin with a small amount of the butter. Spoon the golden syrup into the greased basin.

2 Cream the remaining butter with the sugar until light and fluffy. Gradually add the eggs, beating well after each addition.

3 Sift the flour and baking powder together, then fold into the creamed mixture using a large metal spoon. Add enough water to give a soft, dropping consistency. Spoon into the heatproof basin and smooth the surface.

4 Cover the basin with microwave-proof clingfilm, leaving a small space to let air escape. Microwave on HIGH power for 4 minutes, then remove the sponge from the microwave oven and leave to stand for 5 minutes, while it continues to cook.

5 Turn the sponge out on to a warmed serving plate. Serve with custard.

* This recipe is cooked in a microwave

# almost instant toffee pudding

£

- serves 6
- prepared in 10 mins
- cooks in 15 mins

2 eggs
100 ml/3½ fl oz milk
pinch of ground cinnamon
6 slices of white bread,
 crusts removed
115 g/4 oz unsalted butter

1 tbsp sunflower oil
55 g/2 oz muscovado sugar
4 tbsp golden syrup

1 Using a fork, beat the eggs with 6 tablespoons of the milk and the cinnamon in a large, shallow dish. Cut the bread into triangles and place in the dish, in batches if necessary, to soak for 2–3 minutes.

2 Melt half the butter with half the oil in a heavy-based frying pan. Add the bread triangles, in batches, and cook for 2 minutes on each side, or until golden brown, adding a little more butter and oil as necessary. Remove with a fish slice, drain on kitchen paper, transfer to serving plates and keep warm.

3 Add the remaining butter and milk to the frying pan with the sugar and golden syrup and cook, stirring constantly, until hot and bubbling. Pour the toffee sauce over the bread triangles and serve.

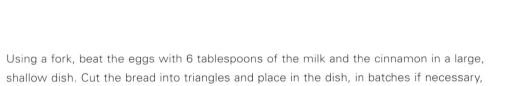
1

2

3

# baked pears in cinnamon

- serves 4
- prepared in 10 mins
- cooks in 30 mins

**4 ripe pears**
**2 tbsp lemon juice**
**50 g/1¾ oz light muscovado**
  **sugar**
**1 tsp ground cinnamon**
**55 g/2 oz low-fat spread**
**450 ml/16 fl oz low-fat custard**
**strips of lemon rind, to decorate**

1 Preheat the oven to 200°C/ 400°F/Gas Mark 6. Core and peel the pears, then slice in half lengthways and brush all over with the lemon juice. Place the pears, cored-side down, in a small non-stick roasting tin.

2 Place the sugar, cinnamon and low-fat spread in a small saucepan and heat gently, stirring constantly, until the sugar has melted. Keep the heat low to prevent too much water evaporating from the low-fat spread. Spoon the mixture over the pears, then bake in the preheated oven, occasionally spooning the sugar mixture over the fruit, for 20–25 minutes, or until the fruit is tender and golden.

3 Heat the custard until piping hot and spoon over the bases of 4 warmed dessert plates. Arrange 2 pear halves on each plate, decorate with strips of lemon rind and serve immediately.

1                    2                    2

# quick tiramisù

£££

- serves 4
- prepared in 15 mins
- cooks in 0 mins

225 g/8 oz mascarpone or full-
   fat soft cheese
1 egg, separated
2 tbsp natural yogurt
2 tbsp caster sugar

2 tbsp dark rum
2 tbsp strong black coffee
8 sponge finger biscuits
2 tbsp grated plain dark
   chocolate

1 Place the cheese in a large bowl, add the egg yolk and yogurt and, using a wooden spoon, beat until smooth.

2 Using a whisk, whisk the egg white in a separate spotlessly clean, greasefree bowl until stiff but not dry, then whisk in the sugar and carefully fold into the cheese mixture.

3 Spoon half of the mixture into 4 tall sundae glasses.

4 Mix the rum and coffee together in a shallow dish. Dip the sponge fingers briefly into the rum mixture, break them in half or into smaller pieces, if necessary, and divide between the glasses.

5 Stir any of the remaining rum and coffee mixture into the remaining cheese and spoon over the top.

6 Sprinkle with grated chocolate and serve immediately. Alternatively, chill in the refrigerator until required.

# pancake pieces

£

- serves 4
- prepared in 15 mins
- cooks in 10 mins

2 tbsp caster sugar
1 tsp ground cinnamon
125 g/4½ oz plain flour
pinch of salt
2 eggs, lightly beaten
125 ml/4 fl oz milk

400 g/14 oz canned apricot
  halves in syrup
sunflower oil, for brushing

2

1 Place the sugar and cinnamon in a bowl, stir to mix and reserve.

2 Sift the flour and salt into a separate bowl. Whisk the eggs and milk into the flour and continue whisking to make a smooth batter.

3 Drain the apricot halves, reserving the syrup, then whisk the syrup into the batter until combined. Roughly chop the apricots and reserve.

4

4 Heat a large crêpe pan or heavy-based frying pan and brush with oil. Pour in the batter and cook over a medium heat for 4–5 minutes, or until the underside is golden brown. Turn over with a palette knife and cook the second side for 4 minutes, or until golden. Tear the pancake into bite-sized pieces with 2 spoons or forks.

5 Add the apricots to the crêpe pan and heat through briefly. Divide the pancake pieces and apricots between 4 serving plates, sprinkle with the sugar and cinnamon mixture and serve immediately.

5

# apple fritters

**£**

- serves 4
- prepared in 10 mins
- cooks in 10 mins

sunflower oil, for deep-frying
1 large egg
pinch of salt
175 ml/6 fl oz water
55 g/2 oz plain flour
2 tsp ground cinnamon

55 g/2 oz caster sugar
4 eating apples, peeled
  and cored

1 Pour the sunflower oil into a deep-fryer or large, heavy-based saucepan and heat to 180–190°C/350–375°F/Gas Mark 4-5, or until a cube of bread browns in 30 seconds.

2 Meanwhile, using an electric mixer, beat the egg and salt together until frothy, then quickly whisk in the water and flour. Do not overbeat the batter – it doesn't matter if it isn't completely smooth.

2

3 Mix the cinnamon and sugar together in a shallow dish and reserve.

3

4 Slice the apples into 5-mm/¼-inch thick rings. Spear with a fork, 1 slice at a time, and dip in the batter to coat. Add to the hot oil, in batches, and cook for 1 minute on each side, or until golden and puffed up. Remove with a slotted spoon and drain on kitchen paper. Keep warm while you cook the remaining batches. Transfer to a large serving plate, sprinkle with the cinnamon sugar and serve.

4

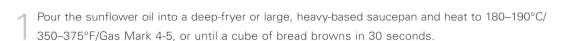
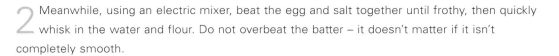

# peach & apple crumble

**££**

- serves 4-6
- prepared in 15 mins
- cooks in 30 mins

1 cooking apple
2 dessert apples
125 ml/4 fl oz cold water
400 g/14 oz canned peach slices
  in fruit juice, drained
85g/3 oz plain flour
55 g/2 oz porridge oats
55 g/2 oz demerara sugar
55 g/2 oz polyunsaturated
  spread
custard made with skimmed
  milk, low-fat natural fromage
  frais or yogurt, to serve

1 Preheat the oven to 190°C/ 375°F/Gas Mark 5. Peel, core and slice the apples and put into a small saucepan with the water. Bring to the boil, then cover and simmer, stirring occasionally, for 4–5 minutes, or until just tender. Remove from the heat and drain away any excess liquid. Stir the drained peach slices into the apple and transfer the fruit to a 1-litre/1½-pint ovenproof dish.

2 Meanwhile, combine the flour, oats and sugar in a mixing bowl. Rub in the spread with your fingertips until the mixture resembles fine breadcrumbs.

3 Sprinkle the crumble topping evenly over the fruit and bake in the preheated oven for 20 minutes, or until golden brown. Serve warm with custard made with skimmed milk, or low-fat natural fromage frais or yogurt. This dessert is best eaten on the day it is made – any leftover crumble should be stored in the refrigerator and consumed within 24 hours.

1          1          2

# index